LOVE YOU & HE WILL TOO

The Smart Woman's Roadmap for Happy, Healthy Relationships

ELIZABETH OVERSTREET

Love You and He Will Too: The Smart Woman's Roadmap for Happy, Healthy Relationships

978-0-9976761-9-8

0-9976761-9-1

Distributed by Bublish, Inc

CONTENTS

INTRODUCTION

I am a relationship investigator. I've been investigating relationships—my own, as well as others'—for decades. I know how to succeed at dating.

Here are the five basic rules to relationship success:

1. Learn to Love Yourself
2. Be Realistic about Your Expectations in a Relationship
3. Stop Being so Damn Picky - No one is Perfect
4. Being in a Relationship is Like Being on a Team
5. Find Healthy Relationships to Model

In listening to my family, friends, and loved ones go through the ups and downs of their relationships, I've learned what works and what doesn't. We are all too hard on ourselves. In fact, we are often hard on ourselves for having specific feelings. We think such feelings are just our own, not shared by others. This is not true.

What I mean by this is we are all human. Each of us has good moments and challenging moments in our interactions with those we love.

However, because of generally accepted perceptions of how a relationship should be, and due to comparing our situation to others, we often get trapped in our feelings as opposed to allowing ourselves to feel the way we need to feel within each of our relationships.

I've been there. You have too. Comparing our own situation to what a friend has or looking at a relationship we perceive to be what we want instead of exploring what we need to be happy with ourselves. Staying in relationships out of comfort, familiarity, obligation, or fear of being alone. I have experienced all of these feelings and watched as others around me struggled with these issues as well.

I don't know about you, but I'm done with that. It doesn't work. It doesn't make my life happier or my relationships better.

Maybe it's time to change the narrative of your story and how you see relationships. But first you must figure out who you are before you eclipse into something with someone else. Another relationship in which you are not fully ready. This is a more difficult path to take versus moving from relationship to relationship. It is easier not to deal with yourself than to fully investigate your feelings, discover who you are, and build yourself up into what you need to be.

THE RELATIONSHIP INVESTIGATOR

I have been married before; I have gone through a divorce. I have had long-term relationships, and I have dated as a single parent. All of these experiences taught me what I need in a relationship. I learned how to value myself before allowing someone else into my space.

I have coached and mentored others who are married, divorced, cohabitating, single, and unhappy. I have discussed and advised, sharing perspectives on dating, love, marriage, and being happy within a relationship.

Relationships are often more complicated and tangled than we imagine. It can be difficult to understand what ties two people together. Sometimes it helps to see things through a different perspective. A new lens.

That's what this book provides for you. A new way of looking at yourself so that you can bring your best dating persona forward. That way, you will be able to attract a partner who is the right one for you, or enhance your current relationship.

This book will help you become a relationship investigator too. Reading it will help you find a relationship that works best for you. The process of finding someone and falling in love should not be a burdensome task. This book will start the dialogue and help you see that no matter who you are, there is someone who will love and accept you unconditionally.

It is likely you have read countless books by the experts on dating and relationships. So now you are reading *this* book. There is a lot of great advice out there on the subject. Maybe too much advice. And it's complicated, lengthy, and time consuming to read and absorb.

This book is different. The goal of this guide is to compile, share, and clarify the top experts' advice. That way, you can use all of it to find the relationship that works for you. This is the fast way to a successful relationship.

Ready? Okay. Let's get you on the right path to relationship success.

GROWING INTO A RELATIONSHIP

One of the most interesting things about humans is our strong desire to connect with others. If you think of it from a symbiotic perspective, you acquire this desire during the time you are in your mother's womb. As you grow and develop as a fetus, you are attached to her in the closest way possible, becoming aware of her voice, heartbeat, and warmth. This in essence is your safety net.

Being delivered from the safety of a mother's body is perhaps one of the most traumatic events we all must experience. The transition from a safe, warm, and cozy environment into the real world is difficult. A mother is most needed by her baby during those early days to nurture and help find one's space in the world.

As each of us grew up, we passed through the same stages: infant, toddler, tween, teen, and young adult to a more mature adult. All this time, we were learning how to be independent; we still craved the warmth, interaction, and bond we shared with mother, and often with dad.

As we mature, we feel a desire to experience this same warmth, interaction, and bond with someone else. This is known as a transfer of love and attachment.

This transference is normal and healthy. As we continue to evolve as independent adults, we seek a connection with someone who understands and loves us for who we are. There is a very powerful connection when we meet someone and interact in a relationship in which we realize they ***get us*** and ***accept us*** for who we are and what we are.

This is exactly what we've been looking for. What *you* have been wanting, possibly your whole life.

This connection is so strong initially that it can make you dive in head first and go deep, expressing emotions you might not know you had. As you go through these feelings with your significant other, experiencing struggles, ups and downs, and immense joy, these feelings form a bond of love.

Love is both a wonderful and scary thing. Allowing yourself to be vulnerable to another person is the ultimate in that you feel the safety net of someone who loves and values you. Yet, it can also be daunting.

There is tremendous social pressure to present yourself at your best at all times to capture the ideal love. This has created an atmosphere in which you must constantly look to up your game, get the best person possible, consider all of your options, and keep up with the latest in relationship advice. All this does is lead you away from the basics of getting the relationship you want. This may lead you to look for unrealistic relationships, sometimes causing you to get involved in unhealthy relationships, and possibly to settle for situations in which you are not truly happy.

THE ONE

The obsession with finding ***the one*** permeates our culture. From the reality shows that paint the fairy tale of idyllic love, TV programs that always show issues happily solved within a one hour window, and the relentless presence of social media depicting the perfect couple, we are bombarded by the idea that there is one person out there for each of us to love. This creates an unrealistic picture of what love is.

This book will dismiss the fairy tales, brush away all the media fantasies, and tell it like it is. That way, you can get back to the basics to get on the best relationship track. This book will help you on your journey to be with the person you are meant to be with while showing you how to focus on what is most important in a relationship.

Remember the five basic rules to relationship success? This is what we will cover in short order:

1. Learn to Love Yourself
2. Be Realistic about Your Expectations in a Relationship
3. Stop Being so Damn Picky – No one is Perfect
4. Being in a Relationship is Like Being on a Team
5. Find Healthy Relationships to Model

CHAPTER 1

First Things First, Learn to Love Yourself

Throughout this book you will see infographics, quotes from psychologists and other dating experts, and other relevant materials. The facts can help to guide and support you as you investigate relationships and forge the path to a successful relationship for yourself.

My goal in this book is to provide you with takeaways about relationships. These will come from the experts in the field of relationships including dating, marriage, and human behavior. I provide you with my own investigations and interpretations of the top experts' advice. I have distilled their books and philosophies for you in this short guide. This will give you a quick reference to the best advice out there on relationships success.

From there, you can investigate and work on your own. Then you too can enter into the relationship which works best for you or you can strengthen your current relationship.

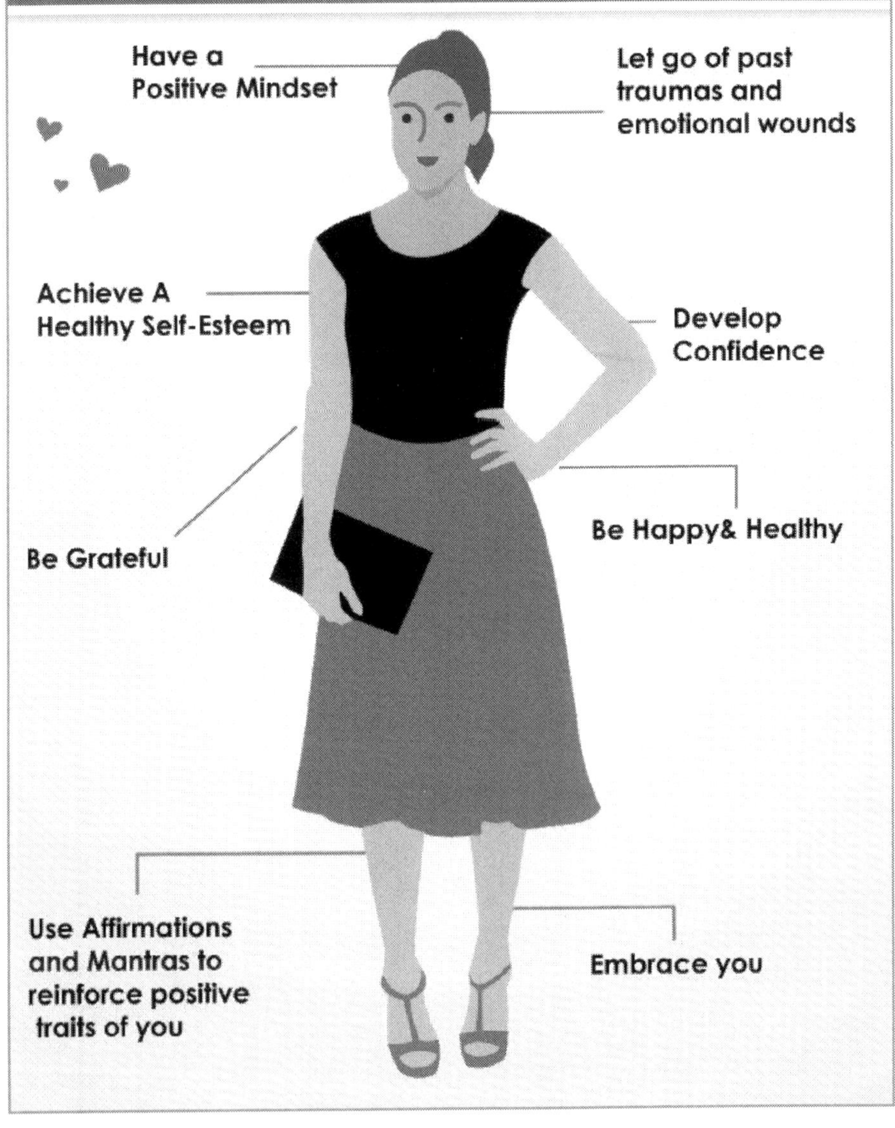
The Pathway to Self-Love
Have a Positive Mindset
Let go of past traumas and emotional wounds
Achieve A Healthy Self-Esteem
Develop Confidence
Be Grateful
Be Happy& Healthy
Use Affirmations and Mantras to reinforce positive traits of you
Embrace you

DR. PHIL ON THE IMPORTANCE OF SELF-LOVE

"The Journey does not begin with you and your partner; it begins with you. What I've discovered with stark and undeniable clarity is that the ones who do well are so in touch with their individual core of consciousness, so aware of their self-worth and their sense of personal value, that they not only treat themselves with enormous self-respect but they inspire others to treat them with equal respect."

—Dr. Phil McGraw, *Relationship Rescue: A Seven-Step Strategy for Reconnecting with Your Partner*

Learn to love you. Learn to love you. Learn to love you.

This is so important I am repeating here like a mantra. Make it YOUR mantra. If you are not in love with you, why in the world should someone else love you? Both strange and good things happen when you learn to accept yourself, flaws and all. It makes you much more attractive and appealing to others.

Have you noticed how you are more drawn to a particular person when you can tell they value themselves? Have you noticed how even their flaws seem attractive and endearing? This may be counterintuitive, but it happens all the time.

Why? Because when you see someone who is comfortable with themselves, even with showing their vulnerabilities, you can see who they really are. When you see someone's authenticity, you automatically hone in on this and it makes the person seem even more attractive. This is because each of us has flaws and faults. These are like the elephant in the room. They stomp around unmentioned and it makes everyone uncomfortable. Unless you embrace them as part of who you are as a person. When you reveal and acknowledge who you are fully, you become more relatable. And when you are more relatable, you become more endearing, attractive, and interesting.

When you are good with you and all aspects of you, people will bond to you, relate to you, and find you more real. Even if you reveal things that may not be so appealing, others will feel compassion for you. This is because every one of us struggles with some kind of self-perceived insecurity, flaw, or weakness, and we all want validation that we are okay despite our imperfections.

Learning to be with yourself and have fun with yourself is ***POWERFUL***. When you fully understand who you are and what you bring to the table by being who you are—along with all the good, the bad, and the ugly—this can make you much more attractive to others. This gives you more appeal than someone who strives to appear perfect.

This is why even superheroes have flaws.

Superman wants to fit in and appear normal to Lois Lane. Batman longs to save the family he feels guilty for losing and laments about what he could have done to change the outcome after losing his parents at a young age. The Incredible Hulk wants to control himself from changing from Bruce Banner; he just wants to be a normal guy. We see these flaws in our favorite superheroes but this does not turn us off. We still admire them. In fact, we respect their bravery even more because we know they are vulnerable. Like us.

DR. PHIL ON WHY YOU ARE NOT ATTRACTING THE PERSON YOU WANT

"Until you begin to live with dignity, respect, and emotional integrity, you will not have that quality and level of interaction with anyone else. As I like to say, you cannot give away what you do not have. If you don't have a pure and healthy love and regard for yourself, how can you possibly give that to anyone else? And if you can't give it to anyone else, then how can you possibly expect to have it reciprocated?"

—Dr. Phil McGraw. *Relationship Rescue: A Seven-Step Strategy for Reconnecting with Your Partner*

In listening to a male perspective on dating one day, I was struck by the following candid observation. The man was speaking about what kind of woman he and other guys find most attractive.

He stated that women are often surprised by guys' choices in mates. This is because guys often date women who are not the most attractive by society's standards. Instead, they are drawn to the woman who feels comfortable with herself and is happy in her own skin.

The reason why this trait is attractive is because the woman is in tune with herself, understands what she will/will not accept, and lives life on her own terms. This means having a man in her life is not something she looks at as a necessity. In her mind, she is okay in her own right, regardless of whether she is with a guy. The guy is the cherry on top in her life, not the ice cream.

This makes sense. When we are happy, we draw positive people and energy to us naturally. In fact, it is effortless. However, when we have too much negative energy, are unsure or insecure, the opposite happens. We draw a different type of energy into our circle and people appear who carry this same type of energy.

Think back over your dating history. Think about the best relationships you ever had. What was your frame of mind during those time periods? Who were you attracting? What were their traits?

Now, think back to a negative relationship and what your frame of mind was like during that period of time. What types of people did you attract? What were they like?

Like most people, I have experienced both sides of the coin. When my frame of mind about myself was not in the right place, I attracted partners who were not good for me. I refer to this period of dating time as my ***dating dark ages.***

The next time you are at a party, take notice of which woman or man receives the most attention. Maybe it will surprise you. Because it may not be the best looking woman or the guy with the perfect body. Rather, it is the average looking person, the one who is able to be him- or herself. This is an energy presented which makes others want to be around them. This energy comes from the confidence of knowing who they are, what they bring to the table, their value. And this creates an irresistible force field. Their magnetism draws an array of suitors to them.

Someone who is not confident is not likely to approach someone who is confident because they know they have to bring their A game. So keep in mind the energy you project becomes literally the company you keep.

You can see this for yourself. Next time you are at work function, bar, club, or party, be observant. Do a little investigative work. Notice who catches your eye, the person you think will shake up the room, anyone there who seems to exude the attraction energy. Now, watch what happens to that individual. Pay attention to who interacts with them, the people who surround them, and how much attention they receive.

See? It's not what you look like but how you like yourself.

It's clear the take away here is to love yourself. Be comfortable with the skin you are in, embrace and be confident about your flaws. You are enough, you have value on your own. Because a relationship will not complete you. A good and healthy relationship will only serve to complement who you already are.

As Dr. Phil says, "Reconnecting with your partner cannot happen if you do not connect with yourself first." I would take it a step further. Reconnecting or connecting with a partner or potential suitor cannot happen if you do not know yourself first.

SELF-LOVE MANTRA:

I love myself completely for who I am and how I am. I may be different from others, but that is okay because I am okay with me.

The Ideal Relationship

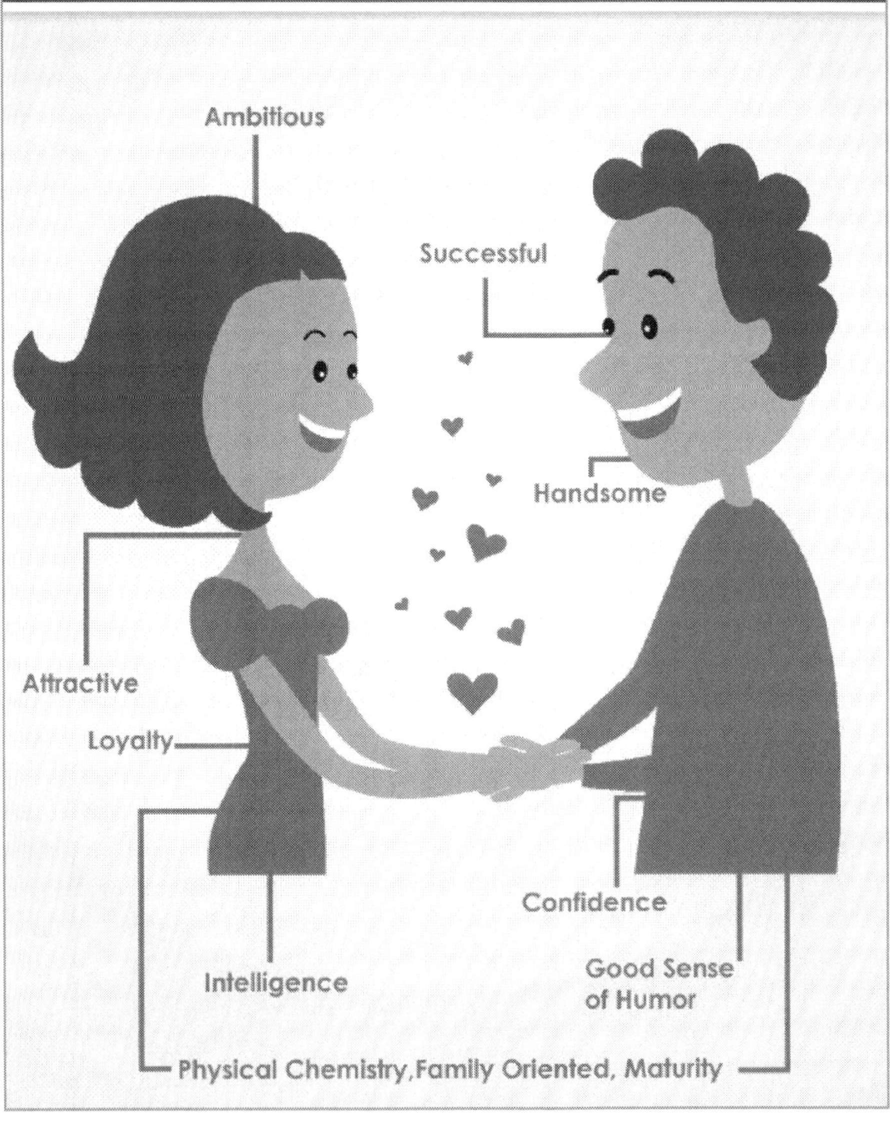

CHAPTER 2

Be Realistic about Your Expectations in a Relationship

> "We must be willing to learn our spouse's or significant other's primary love language if we are to be effective communicators of love."
>
> —Gary Chapman, *The 5 Love Languages: The Secret to Love that Lasts*

What is a love language and what does it have to do with setting expectations in a relationship?

Understanding and practicing you and your significant other's love language can significantly impact your relationship. Gary Chapman's book on the five Love Languages is a great read for those starting out and for those in relationships. His approach can help you to determine what drives you within a relationship.

The concept of the five Love Languages is based on the fact that you are moved by specific actions of your significant other. This makes you more vested in the relationship with this person.

The love languages are:

1. Words of Affirmation;
2. Quality Time;
3. Receiving Gifts;
4. Acts of Service; and
5. Physical Touch.

Affirmation means receiving positive feedback from your partner. Quality Time means valuing time spent with your partner. Receiving Gifts from your partner is love spoken because the gift can be an acknowledgement of how deeply your partner cares for you. Acts of Service are those things you do that show how you value the other person. This can mean cleaning the house, providing needed alone time, taking a duty or responsibility off one another's plate, or other acts of kindness. Physical Touch means having a partner show affection via hand holding, touching, kissing and hugging, as well as sexual intimacy.

Once you and your partner understand what drives one another, this knowledge increases the closeness of your relationship as well as strengthening your bond.

Seem simple? It is. Often we naturally use the love languages early on in our relationships. However, as time goes on and the relationship matures, we stop doing those things which initially kept the relationship close, fresh, and exciting. Understanding your love language and that of your potential or current partner strengthens the relationship for the long-term and keeps what Dr. Chapman calls your love tank on full.

This concept resonates and is a difference maker in a relationship.

INTERPRETATION MODE

Sometimes relationships are hard because we make them hard. We make assumptions about our partners rather than ask them directly about their intentions. When our significant other exhibits a certain behavior, fails to take a specific action towards us, or acts a certain way, we may go into our own ***interpretation mode***.

What does this mean? It means you interpret the other person's actions based on how you would feel or act instead of asking why the person exhibited the specific action.

For example, say your lover fails to acknowledge your birthday in the way you are used to having your birthday acknowledged. You may automatically assume their intentions were negative, bad, thoughtless, and unloving. You feel hurt, rejected, and unloved.

But is this really the case? Or are your feelings centered on your own interpretations and expectations? Why not ask your partner why they made the choice to celebrate or ignore your birthday in this way? They may have a good reason. Maybe they were actually trying to please you, or this is what they did growing up in their family, or they believed it was what you wanted.

We all tend to see things through our own prism. This is how we live, experience, and understand things.

However, you can learn a lot when you step outside of your own prism and look at the world through a different lens.

A small action like this can start you down a different road. You may begin to rely on more realistic expectations in a relationship. This is the path to success.

Think of your parents and their relationship with you. They may know you better than anyone else does. Yet, you probably have times in which you feel like they do not know you at all. This feeling resonates during the teenage years, and may remain in adulthood.

Compare this with someone who is in a relationship with you. They have known you for a comparatively short period of time. Yet, you have expectations that this person will be able to figure you out. You give them hints, limited interactions, and non-verbal clues. And you expect them to know what you want from them at all times.

Kinda unfair, don't you think?

BITTER VERSUS SWEET

However, it *is* important to set expectations in a relationship. You should discuss with your partner where you want to head in your relationship, your values, how you want to raise kids if you have them, whether you want to be monogamous, and other essential issues. If you do not discuss these things, this is a sure way to have relationship woes. These are factors which will place you on the same journey or make you run on opposite paths.

You should not expect your partner to understand your feelings automatically, especially in the beginning. He or she will not know exactly what to do each and every time to make you happy. If you are disappointed when they don't live up to your unrealistic expectations, this will set you up for a ***bitter relationship***.

People in successful relationships have found that having a visual list of their non-negotiables helped. This list enabled them to recognize the traits and expectations they had in mind for a relationship.

You might want to make this kind of list for yourself. The list can be static, and understanding what is important to you will help you to stay away from potential partners who do not meet the standards you require for a relationship.

For example, say you want to have children and you meet someone who does not want to have kids. With your list in mind, you can avoid getting involved. Instead of attempting to change the other person's mind, you can turn your focus to someone else. A potential partner who is more aligned to your own goals. This can only occur if you already know ahead of time that having kids is one of your non-negotiables.

We all have heard the horror stories. We all know people who have sacrificed their non-negotiables and ended up with someone who is not a good fit. We all know sad people who feel cheated, not fulfilled.

This is not the path to a healthy relationship.

Make your list and check it twice. Don't look for someone who meets your expectations until your list is done. That way, you can hit the ground running when you meet the person with whom you want to spend your life.

RELATIONSHIP REALISM MANTRA:

I will set realistic expectations in my relationship.

professional SPORTSCAR intelligent charming SPORTSCAR professional POLITE wealthy
POPULAR devoted understanding understanding PROFESSIONAL
understanding understanding
WEALTHY professional
CARING businessman
WISE businessman polite
kind CHARMING
professional BUSINESSMAN
HELPFUL
tall romantic charismatic
tall popular tall
tall HANDSOME
INTELLIGENT
TALL devoted
WISE
wise helpful
kind POPULAR
businessman
stylish caring
kind MACHO
gentle romantic
athletic
witty INTELLIGENT HELPFUL
wise Handsome
athletic
mansion smart
stylish mansion
athletic
friendly athletic polite
smart
macho intelligent KIND
polite
wise
INTELLIGENT PASSIONATE
gentle HANDSOME
friendly athletic FRIENDLY witty
stylish intelligent smart
athletic businessman passionate
intelligent Handsome passionate
BUSINESSMAN DEVOTED smart
funny athletic intelligent
WISE helpful Handsome passionate
stylish businessman friendly passionate
PASSIONATE

?

businessman charismatic
charming
professional charismatic
muscular
popular romantic POLITE CARING charismatic
understanding
BUSINESSMAN charismatic helpful
MUSCULAR
WEALTHY
professional
TALL POLITE tall
loving loving
KIND stylish
charismatic
charming polite
athletic
PROFESSIONAL influential
sportscar
friendly
sportscar caring
tall funny wise
MANSION WITTY KIND
INFLUENTIAL friendly
romantic witty
charismatic gentle
INFLUENTIAL STYLISH
INFLUENTIAL
kind WITTY INFLUENTIAL
MUSCULAR sportscar
mansion muscular funny
gentle INFLUENTIAL influential
MANSION funny sportscar
devoted
ROMANTIC charismatic understanding
ROMANTIC loving sportscar witty
MANSION funny WEALTHY influential
MACHO understanding muscular witty
influential CHARMING devoted mansion

CHAPTER 3

Stop Being So Damn Picky – No one is Perfect

In the age of high tech dating with access to a multitude of dating websites, apps, and social media, it seems easier than ever before to be choosy about partners. With such a ready availability of so many potential partners, you may find that you are even more picky than usual when choosing someone to date.

This kind of selectivity may be overdone, eliminating the best relationships from your list of options.

Did you make the list of non-negotiables? If so, you are well aware of the traits you want in a relationship partner. However, take another look at your list. If you have too many qualifications, you may be overlooking potential partners who could make you happy.

Time to redo your list?

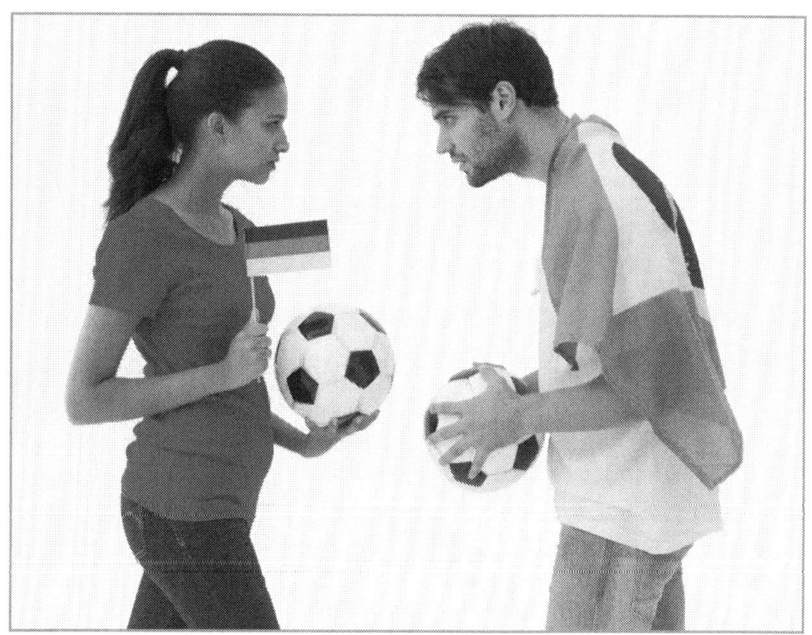

PERFECT VERSUS PERFECT FOR YOU

The key is to be realistic. You may need to let go of some of your requirements. Do you really need a mate with Barbie doll measurements? Does he have to drive a specific car or work in a specific profession? Is that particular salary range a must? Are the height and weight really non-negotiable? Such picky standards can be tangibles that limit your options.

It is important to have standards, to know what you need. But this should be tempered with a dose of realism. After all, ***you are not perfect.*** No one is!

We all have our imperfections, our areas of weakness. Each of us has our appealing and not so appealing traits. Why would we expect to find a partner who is perfect if we aren't ourselves?

We all need to give ourselves the time and space to work on our weaknesses, to grow and evolve. And we need to remember this when looking for a significant other. Pay attention to the little things, but don't overanalyze them. Don't be too kneejerk about rejecting someone. Take your time and give them ample consideration.

So, say you meet someone and he is nice, easy to talk to, and is enjoying a successful career. But he does not have all the physical attributes of what you regard as your ideal type. If he vibes with you in the other areas, are you going to sacrifice the connection because he isn't as tall or handsome as you might want? Because if you already dated other men who *were* tall and handsome and you failed to connect with them on an emotional level or had little in common with them, wouldn't it be a good idea to try something different?

In matters of the heart, you must weigh the total picture. It is important to see a person for who they are wholly, not just in pieces. Even though the natural tendency is to focus on the external first, then the internal. We judge the book by its cover, sometimes too quickly. Because in the long-term, who the person is, how you interact with them, and how they complement you will be what brings totality to the relationship—along with the external traits like height, weight, measurements, salary, and looks. It is the internal that will drive the relationship for the long run.

Don't get me wrong. External is important too. Most of the initial attraction between two people is physical in nature, and that is normal. But the external component will fade eventually and can be altered suddenly due to a change in health, accidents, aging, and other factors. And looking at the other side of the coin, what if *you* are the person who is valued only on an external level? Do you want to be with someone who is just into your looks or income rather than your most valuable assets?

Think of it from this perspective. External plays some significance but is short-term. Internal is long-term and indicative of how a couple will evolve in a relationship. We all want to be loved for who we really are. Who we are inside, our internal factors, are what determine who we will be in the long-term.

We've all dated people who felt we lacked qualities they thought they needed for the long term. Maybe they initially thought we were not tall or thin enough, kinda boring, or nothing jumped out and made them go *wow*.

However, they gave you additional chances and found you to be more likeable as time progressed. That chemistry of immediate attraction does not always occur with the best relationship partners. It happens more naturally with some people, and it does not always happen as quickly as you would like it to.

THE IT FACTOR

There are other factors which play into your attraction to someone. One of these is the ***it factor***. You know, that special trait someone has that draws you closer, the one you just can't explain. But when you feel it, it just feels right. You feel comfortable, unguarded, and in tune. This ***it factor*** magnifies the other feelings you have for the person. It seems like they are someone you can be around for the longer term.

The ***it factor*** is usually immediate.

However, there's also the other side of the coin. Many solid relationships exist in which couples did not at first think it would work out for them, but over time proved to be successful. This is why it is always a good idea to be open and take it slow. If the ***it factor*** is apparent, great. However, if it is not there at first, why not give the relationship time anyway? And see what happens.

Relationships are strange in that way. They can start off fast or slow and still have positive outcomes. It is too easy to eliminate someone quickly when you first start dating. Better to take time to see what develops. And if you are already in a relationship, one that needs work, why not continue to give it a chance? Try to remember why you were initially attracted. Then go from there.

In relationships, there's always room for growth. And improvement. There's the take- away.

So, be open. Know what you want, yet understand you might meet a diamond in the rough. We all can appreciate the person who is there for us when we are in the beginning stages of building something. Then, after the relationship takes off, you are likely to be rewarded for your patience and support during the process. We all value a partner who can be supportive, love us for who we are, help us to evolve, and provide constructive feedback. We all need someone who can be both a friend *and* a lover.

And this can mean a relationship that is perfect. Not perfect, but perfect for our own individual needs.

ACCEPTANCE MANTRA:

I will be picky, just not too damn picky when choosing my mate!

CHAPTER 4
Being in a Relationship is Like Being on a Team

"The quality of a relationship is a function of the extent to which it is built on a solid underlying friendship and meets the needs of the two people involved."

—Dr. Phil McGraw, *Relationship Rescue: A Seven-Step Strategy for Reconnecting with Your Partner*

Everyone agrees on how great it can be when a relationship is on fire. This kind of passion is fun and the relationship can be liberating, carefree, and easy. The challenge for most of us is when this same relationship changes. Like when the relationship goes through a major challenge.

When you are clashing with your significant other, going through a particularly difficult time, or not agreeing about anything, it can be tough to stay the course. During these times, it is so easy for you to think you want to leave the relationship. But you might want to make sure you are leaving because the situation is toxic or unhealthy, not because you hit a speed bump on your relationship course.

Think of it this way. You and your significant other are a team. Teams stay together through it all. When it is good, they celebrate. When it is bad, they cry, they support and comfort each other through the pain. When things are okay, well, they are okay. But, as any team knows, in order to win, you are going to go through some losses. These low times can be looked at as a learning period. Such times can help prepare you to handle and navigate the wins.

Unfortunately, one does not exist without the other. The point is this: no relationship is static. Your relationship will not stay the same. This is good because if it did, no matter how good it was, either or both of you would grow bored with it.

BE A TEAM PLAYER

When one team member is down, it is going to affect the others. One person may not be as attuned to the others. Disagreements may erupt more easily. This is all part of team play. It is part of being in a relationship.

What is important to remember is that you are a TEAM: ***Together Everyone Achieves More.*** When the team is struggling or trying to figure out something, charting the course together makes the process less formidable.

Rather than stepping back during these times, challenges, losses, and arguments mark a good time for you to step up. Help your partner chart the course.

Be supportive, loving, and understanding. Life happens in cycles so it is natural for you to have your ups and downs. He or she may need you to stand fast; and you may need him or her to do so one day as well. Working together can be a powerful thing. When one of you is there to help the other, this strengthens the relationship.

One of my friends has been married a long time. He jokes about how he always tries to "put money in the bank" when it comes to his wife. What he means by this is he takes the opportunity to do thoughtful things for her. He buys flowers, takes her out to dinner, and tells her she looks good. He takes on tasks, and gives her breaks from the everyday chores. By doing these things, he's being smart. He knows this builds good will in their relationship. He also realizes how this softens the rough edges when times are not as good. During the rough patches, his kind gestures are remembered and help to keep their relationship steady and balanced.

This is the smart approach to a partnership. To team play. You will always have ups and downs in your life, and you will experience them in any relationship. Most couples admit they have experienced these changing flows within their relationship. Such challenges are to be expected. And they require that we remain team players as we work to become winners again.

Teamwork will always make a better relationship. That's the take-away. And teams can accomplish more than individuals. Teams create a stronger entity every time. This is because when you work as a team, you have more brainpower, you have collaboration, and you allow for the diversity of thought that leads to better play, better solutions.

TEAM BUILDING MANTRA:

In my relationship, if I focus on us then we will accomplish much more.

CHAPTER 5

Find Healthy Relationships to Model

"There is not some etched-in-stone right way to be in a relationship. What is important is that you find ways of being together that work for you."

—Dr. Phil McGraw. *Relationship Rescue: A Seven-Step Strategy for Reconnecting with Your Partner*

The great thing about your relationship is that you can create your own story. And if you are not able to figure out your own story, then you can always learn about what others have done to create successful relationships.

Once you have completed the first four rule of success in relationships, you are well along on the path. You are loving yourself, exhibiting positive energy, attracting good people with good vibes. You are being realistic about relationships and tempering your expectations.

You are giving it time and space to evolve. You know what you want and what your non-negotiables are in the partner you will choose. If you are single, you are being more open and you have stopped being so damn picky. You have viable choices. If you are already in a relationship, you are ready to move ahead. Maybe your relationship hit a low note, or maybe you lost your way. But with the first four rules in mind, you are working toward rebuilding your relationship with your partner.

No matter what your status, you realize that your relationship takes teamwork, an understanding of who the other individual is and how they relate to you, and a willingness to work hard to make your relationship succeed.

FINDING GOOD ROLE MODELS

If you come from a family background with divorce or trauma, then obviously you do not want to model the relationship behavior you observed growing up. You want a partnership that is healthier and longer lasting. Fortunately, you can learn from other relationships besides your parents'. You can be a relationship investigator and see who is doing it right.

Start by identifying some of the healthy relationships you've observed in your life. Think about the couples you know who have a tight bond and mutual understanding. There are probably some couples you want to be like, others you do not want to model. You know the difference between a healthy relationship and a toxic one.

Just like when you start a job and you want to do your best and be at the top of your game, you can seek out someone who is successful to mentor you. Or you can model the behavior of someone who is highly accomplished in their relationship.

If there is a couple in your life who seems to have figured it out and they have the type of relationship you would like to have, investigate. Observe their behaviors and interactions. Don't just pay attention to the good stuff. Look at how they handle the tougher parts of their relationship. This is where you will start to understand people and how they interact with each other.

How do they manage the parenting of their kids? How do they handle it when they disagree on a topic? How do they communicate this to each other? Are they respectful? Do they display affection? Are they complimentary to each other? How do their differences help make their relationship better?

No couple is *on* 24/7. And no matter what anyone says, there is always going to be some conflict in a relationship. Some conflicts go unresolved. And successful couples can live with this.

There are telltale signs for when a couple is happily cohabitating and when this is not the case. Pay close attention. When you observe what people do versus what they say, things will become clear. Pay attention to body language and other non-verbal cues. A strong indicator of a healthy relationship is each person being who they are and not altering their personality.

Many years ago I attended a holiday party for one of my jobs. We had been told to bring our significant other. I could tell who was comfortable with their spouse. These individuals behaved the same way they did at work with their colleagues. Others did not, and seemed uncomfortable with their significant other in the social situation.

One guy I worked with was a huge flirt in the office. He was harmless, but flirty, a big jokester. When I interacted with him and his wife at the party, he continued to display his flirtatious behaviors. Disrespectful? No, because she laughed too. That was who he was, and she had accepted that about him. In fact, this might have been what drew her to him, the *it factor* for her. She told me she knew his heart was in the right place with her.

I realized this was a dynamic in their relationship, one which worked for them. Each couple is its own entity. Each couple has their own way of interacting, understanding, and relating to one another.

At this same party, I observed the other couples. I could tell which ones were not attuned to each other, who seemed tense around their partner, and who wasn't comfortable with interacting or communicating. I found this fascinating.

RELATIONSHIPS THAT WORK

Role models are out there. You may have some in mind. So, investigate. Watch them, then use what you think may work for you and your potential or current significant other.

Be sure to exercise some caution here. No couple has a perfect relationship. And that is important to realize as you observe them in action. Ignore the little things while you pay close attention to the more important things such as the way they handle their ups and downs and how they navigate difficult situations and circumstances.

This can give you some solid ideas on how you and your significant other can handle both the good and the bad times in your own relationship. And don't use this as a be-all approach. Instead, customize what may work for you and your significant other.

There is little rhyme or reason to relationships. They are a mystery, like love. Nobody really knows what makes some relationships successful and others a failure. And there is no one size fits all that works for everyone. Each relationship has its own rhythm.

Be careful not to judge someone else's relationship. Instead, try to understand how each relationship is unique to the parties involved. Ask questions. How do you do it? How do you make your relationship work? Your investigations will pay off for your own future success.

We all may struggle to keep our relationships going. But if we are more transparent and honest about this, we might be able to help each other through.

HEALTHY RELATIONSHIP MANTRA:

I will model healthy relationships and customize what works best for me and my partner. No relationship is perfect. My goal is to learn from others in order to strengthen my own relationship.

****

5 RULES
TO FIND
THE RIGHT ONE
AND MAKE IT WORK

So that's it. The five rules to a successful relationship. That's why this is a *fast* guide to the relationship you want. A quick and easy read.

It's up to you now to do the work required.

Relationships are not easy. That is why they are called relation-ships. How you relate to another person can change from day to day. Your relationship can be rough sailing or steady going or somewhere in between, depending on the day. The key is learning to navigate, working to understand you and your significant other, and being able to stay the course whenever you charter rough waters.

I hope you can use the material I have provided here as you work toward the relationship you want. Repeat your mantras. Work on your list. Investigate relationships. And remember the five rules.

Good luck!

REFERENCE BOOKS ON RELATIONSHIPS

Phil McGraw, *Relationship Rescue: A Seven-Step Strategy for Reconnecting with Your Partner*

HACHETTE BOOKS, 2001

Dr. Phil's approach to relationships is similar to his approach to counseling. He is all about accountability, taking charge of your life, and changing yourself in order to positively change a relationship. This involves helping people to change behaviors and habits which are self-destructive. Once this occurs, people are able to diagnose, repair, and maintain their relationships. Dr. Phil's approach is to provide clear steps which will reconnect individuals in a relationship. The end goal of relationship rescue is to provide readers with an opportunity to have a relationship that is meaningful for both parties.

Dr. Phil is a world-renowned relationship expert and well-respected psychologist. Some of the ideas he suggests in this book are relevant. I agree with Dr.

Phil that you must first work on yourself, because understanding and being in tune with who you are helps in who you attract and how you deal with your relationship.

But there are areas of the book with which I respectfully disagree. First, we are not all the same. We react to different scenarios differently, and these differences are not all gender based. Sometimes there are inexplicable reasons why we may not be in tune with someone and unhappy with them. That is our intuition and emotional intelligence speaking. It is important, therefore, to consider how we look at relationships. Some are meant for the short-term, while others may be more long-term. We learn from each relationship, but we must be sure to evaluate our relationships so that we can find one that is healthy and fulfilling, and energizes us in the long-term.

John Gray, *Men Are From Mars, Women Are From Venus*

HARPER COLLINS, 1992

Dr. Gray focuses on improving the way men and women communicate by acknowledging the different styles females and males use to communicate. He uses the analogy of Martians and Venusians, how they meet and have successful and happy relationships by accepting each other's differences. However, when the Martians and Venusians come to Earth, they forget they are from different planets. And they evolve into human men and women.

This metaphor serves to illustrate the common differences between men and women which interfere with fulfilling and loving relationships, and he uses it to promote the concept of developing a better understanding between couples. In my opinion, however, Dr. Gray's book generalizes too much about women and men. Even though men and women may respond differently in relationships, the bridge of feelings, emotions, and communication is closer than we think.

Relying on gender-based stereotypes does not help us to move closer to the opposite sex. We have lots of depth and breadth, whether we are male or female. This makes us unique, complex, and interesting all at the same time. So, instead of generalizing that someone will act or be a certain way because they are a female or male, more attention should be focused on who the person is as an individual.

Steve Harvey, *Act Like A Woman, Think Like A Man*

AMISTAD, 2009

Steve Harvey has spent years as a radio personality and talk show host speaking with women about relationships. Over the years, he determined women were in the dark about understanding men and why they exhibit certain behaviors. In his book, he focuses on the importance of understanding a man's psyche, figuring out what is important to him, and determining what he is seeking in a relationship. The book provides perspectives on why men cheat, the things a woman should do before she becomes emotionally invested in a man, how to strategize in a relationship in order to get married, how to make oneself more desirable, and other practical tips.

The book is a simplistic approach to understanding dating, relationships, and the female/male dynamic. Though there are many nuggets in this book, much of the material is outdated and old-fashioned. Since the financial gap between men and women has changed over time, so have relationships. Since today's women have more education and freedom, they have more options. Women may choose to put career first rather than adopting the traditional path to marriage and children. Thus, this book fails to emphasize what is important in a relationship to today's women.

If a partner is not up to date on what you want or is too restrictive with who you are, this person is not the one for you. This is tantamount to you giving away the power of you. Today's woman does not want to do this. Strong within the power of herself, she is more adamant about controlling the physical and emotional access provided to a man.

Greg Behrendt and Liz Tuccillo,
He's Just Not That Into You

GALLERY BOOKS, 2004.

Based on a popular "Sex and the City" episode, this book focuses on how to tell if a guy is interested in you by observing his actions. The authors' communication style is tough, direct, with common sense advice for getting out of any relationship which is not working for you.

One recurring theme throughout the book is the fact that women tend to make excuses for men who are not stepping up in a relationship with us for various reasons. However, at the end of the day, if a guy is into you, he will do what it takes to have a relationship. If not, he won't because "He's Just Not That Into You."

The authors' goal is to let women know that they should not waste their time justifying a man's lack of attention and effort in a relationship. The communication of a man in a relationship is simple and is dictated by his actions toward you. Those actions are either engaging with you, adjusting to make you happy, or passive and dismissive of you.

You have to have a sense of humor to understand this book, which is comical, whimsical, and straightforward at the same time. The authors advise us not to overthink a scenario. When a relationship flows naturally, the relationship develops, and people will naturally begin to talk about commitment, next steps, and making plans.

I suggest you also pay attention to the actions and what a potential partner is communicating. If a person tells you they do not want a serious relationship, don't waste your time trying to be the one that changes his or her mind. If they constantly play you off or cancel plans with you, you are not a priority in their life. So, don't make them a priority in yours.

Sometimes authors generalize too much about what the sexes do in relationships. Men and women are not one dimensional. If we were, our relationships would be a lot easier.

Gary Chapman, *The 5 Love Languages: The Secret to Love that Lasts*

NORTHFIELD PUBLISHING, 2009

Dr. Chapman's book teaches readers how to keep their love tank full by doing things that play directly to their love language. Since each of us has a primary love language, when you speak in someone else's love language, they are highly responsive. When dating someone, we intuitively perform actions to express how we feel and how we care. Lots of times these are actions to please that individual or make them happy. The book articulates why we are so responsive to someone in a relationship when they hit on our specific love language: Affirmation, Service, Affection, Time, Gifts.

This is excellent advice worth noting and practicing in relationships. However, be aware that you may have more than one love language.

Dr. Chapman also advises that even when someone is not respecting you, you need to step up to the plate and recognize their love language to rectify the matter. I would have to respectfully disagree with this. If someone does not respect you and is emotionally abusive of you, you need to get counseling to resolve the matter, or move on. There are limits to every relationship and emotional, physical, or toxic relationships which hamper your emotional or physical being are ones in which you should not waste your time.

Dr. Chapman also makes some generalizations about women and men that I find inaccurate (such as men want sex but women just want to cuddle). Some men are more sensitive and emotional than women. And some women value sexuality more in a given relationship. So, to generalize that men or women are more likely to have specific love language is limited thinking.

However, recognizing an individual for who they are will help you to understand them. Using their love language or love languages will enhance your relationship and make it work better for both of you.

ACKNOWLEDGEMENTS

I have always been intrigued with dating and relationships and the dynamics that attract one person to another. My parents have been married for over fifty years, and I was married for seven years and in a long-term relationship for ten. I learned a lot through being single, being married, coming out of a divorce, dealing with a break up, and jumping back into the dating pool. I would like to thank my parents for their modeling, my former partners for their lessons in relationships (what to do and what not to do), and my friends and relatives for allowing me to be a relationship investigator.

A special thank you to my daughter, who supported me and told me to stick with the writing. Her encouragement helped me to bring this book to fruition.

Additional thanks to my editor Virginia Aronson and writing coach Melissa G Wilson. They have helped to guide, encourage, and provide support to me through this journey of getting my thoughts on paper. Writing this book has proved to be cathartic, and the result is a reminder of how much I enjoy writing.

Made in the USA
Lexington, KY
22 July 2017